T0209566

BAPTISM

A Quest for Truth

COLE PARSLEY

WESTBOW
PRESS®
A DIVISION OF THOMAS NELSON
& ZONDERVAN

WestBow Press books may be ordered through booksellers or by contacting:

WestBow Press
A Division of Thomas Nelson & Zondervan
1663 Liberty Drive
Bloomington, IN 47403
www.westbowpress.com
844-714-3454

All scripture quotations are taken from The Holy Bible, English
Standard Version® (ESV®), Copyright © 2001 by Crossway,
a publishing ministry of Good News Publishers. All rights reserved.

ISBN: 978-1-6642-6549-3 (sc)
ISBN: 978-1-6642-6548-6 (hc)
ISBN: 978-1-6642-6550-9 (e)

Library of Congress Control Number: 2022908259

Print information available on the last page.

WestBow Press rev. date: 05/19/2022

CONTENTS

PREFACE

My conlcusions on baptism do not come from a childhood of indoctrination. I did not grow up in the Churches of Christ, or the Christian church, or any other church with a high view of baptism. My parents/grandparents never nurtured me into "correct doctrine" on the topic. As this book showcases, I do believe that baptism is for the forgiveness of sins, but I did not always believe that. Here is my story. This is how it all happened.

It was a late night in the middle of Fall 2015. I stared at the ceiling hoping and begging for sleeps sweet embrace. After hours of tossing and turning, I finally approached God in prayer, and that prayer would not only bring peace which transcends all understanding, but it also would drastically change my life forever. This did not all start with just one sleepless night. These were countless sleepless nights and months of unrest both spiritually and physically. I was a mess as

I asked myself over and over what God's plan was for me. I was in college at the time, and my pursuit in the study of Nutrition was no longer fulfilling.

There was an unrest in my soul over this. It was not simply a career change, but God was communicating too me. Deep down I think I knew what He wanted, but I did not want to accept it. That night in prayer, however, I did accept it, and I felt God's peace which only comes through the power of The Spirit. I remember crying that night as I stood outside in my back yard looking up at the stars. It was over, the torment in my soul seized. I was terrified of the future, "How am I supposed to pursue ministy when I'm terrified of any public speaking whatsoever?", I asked myself. Despite this fear, I was at peace, and yes, it is possible to experience both.

There was a new problem that presented itself that I would spend half a year trying to sort out. If I was going to pursue ministry, then I would need to pick a school. Every school, however, is governed by a specific denomination, and I knew that whichever school I picked would likely lead to my views being changed, and to me pursuing a church/school for work that was in that school's denomination. With this in mind, I decided to wipe the slate clean in regards to my biblical beliefs (or try to at least), and to question everything and to try and learn as much as I could about denominations, their beliefs, and which one was "correct".

I studied relentlessly over those six months, and I questioned everything. It was a stressful experience. It was also hard because my knowledge was very limited. Finally, however, a minister offered to study with me. His name was Tim Knox.

Tim was a member of the Churches of Christ. He invited me to church, and I remember being deeply offended by that Sunday School lesson taught by Steven Smith. It was on baptism, and how Jesus stated that it was necessary for salvation. "What?! This is heresy, salvation is by faith alone at the point of belief!", I said to myself during the lesson. The thought was probably written all over my face as well. You see, at the time, I thought I really knew something about the bible, but in actuality, I was just getting started.

Later that week Tim invited me to a bible study. We studied for probably three hours one on one. It was a humbling and gut-wrenching experience, though I was not combative, I was deeply offended, not by him, but by the truth. The topic we studied was on baptism.

For three months, I studied and meditated on what the scriptures say concerning baptism. It was hard. I read articles and I asked preachers who belief in faith alone about these passages. I also talked to friends about my studies. It is not fair to say I studied baptism for three months. It is more like I fought against the doctrine of baptism for three months. I did not want to believe it, but I was also not willing to dismiss it and pretend the verses were not there.

It was during my commute to school one morning that I became frightened of my own safety. There was a semi-truck on the road, and I thought, "What if I hit them and died? What would happen to me"? You see I had been baptized at a very young age. I did not understand who Jesus or sin was at the time, or at least I doubted that I did. Would that be good enough?

Later that day, I was baptized for the forgiveness of my sins. It was a hard decision because though I wanted to feel secure in my salvation, I also knew there was no going back. In that moment, I forfeighted my old beliefs in faith alone. I surrendered to that old doctrine which also led to me changing which church I worshipped at. There were people from that church who talked to me on a daily basis, but afterwards stopped talking to me altogether. You see, during these months of studies, I was frequently warned not to do it.

Friends treated me differently. I still remember a super bowl party where I was on the hot seat concerning my new views the entire time. Luckily for me, my immediate family was supportive, but that is not always the case for those who accept baptism as for the forgiveness of sins (more on this later).

This next part may sound unbelievable, but I assure

you it happened. After being baptized, I remember feeling at peace, but also worried. It is one thing to make a decision for yourself, but far different is teaching others this newfound belief. The car ride home was a mix of emotions. Walking into my house, I saw my grandfather who greeted me with a deeply troubled look on his face. Scattered across the kitchen table was about five different pamphlets and books on the topic of baptism. They were opened and moved from the location I previously left them.

"How do I receive forgiveness of sins?", he asked me. At that moment the world seemed to slow down as I thought of how I would answer. There was not a single conversation I had with him on this topic prior. This was hard for me to answer, but I answered the only way I knew how, "You need to believe in Jesus *and be baptized.*" I had only thirty minutes to process my new decision, and yet here I was already affirming what I had come to believe.

The very next day, I was given the opportunity to baptize my grandfather. I did nothing, but respond to him, he did all the studying. Months later, I would also baptize my mother, and then just last year I was able to baptize my brother. Let me be clear, in none of these baptisms did I declare that their previous baptism was "not good enough". There are many who believe that all need to be rebaptized once they learn baptism's true purpose, I am not one of those, as is explained later in this book. I am not against rebaptism, however, if a person's conscience is plaquing them.

Over the last seven years I have received my Bachelor's in Biblical Studies. and I am a couple months away from my Masters in Theological Studies. My conclusions on baptism have not changed. I am passionate about this topic, and I want all Christian's everywhere to understand baptism's biblical purpose.

INTRODUCTION

I am a fan of the fantasy genre in literature, movies, and video games. There is something that is just so exciting about the prospect of a new world with dragons, magic, and mystical creatures. A common theme that runs throughout the fantasy genre is the idea of a "quest." A quest is simply a journey guided by some ultimate objective. All of fantasy has, at its core, this journey, which climaxes in a goal. In Harry Potter, the quest is to defeat Voldemort (the evil wizard who killed Harry's parents). In another young adult fantasy, *Wheel of Time*, the inciting moment of the quest takes place when a group of friends are chased out of their childhood village. The friends gain experience and knowledge through their adventures, indulging their curiosity about the outside world. In short, quests can take any number of forms, but there is always a goal which leads to a reward. This reward is never easy, however; often the "treasure" is guarded by a great peril (e.g. the classic "fire-breathing dragon).

In a quest for truth in the realm of theology, the "journey" is not much different from these stories in fantasy. The difference is that the Christian's treasure is not gold or a princess: but truth. Such truth in Christ is accompanied by great reward. Still, it is hemmed with obstacles and perils, bombarding the searching Christian with doubts. To be specific, there are three broad obstacles to accepting truth. The first is *discerning* whether new information is false or true. The second obstacle is struggling through the mountain of *traditions which impact* how one views a given topic. Finally, the third obstacle is having the *courage to accept and embrace* this new truth of which one is convicted. It is at this third obstacle that most fail. This is the most difficult of the three. This is the dragon waiting at the bottom of the castle. Can you find courage to slay the dragon? Can you find the courage to accept hard truths?

Imagine for a moment being born into a society where, for the last thousand years, everyone has believed the sky is red. One thousand years ago, this society decided that every citizen had to wear glasses which make the sky appear red to every citizen. For the current generation this is a simple fact. It is not disputed, and any thought to the contrary is rejected with incredulous looks and disdain. You know the truth, however, after rebelliously taking your glasses off and seeing that the sky is actually blue. This revelation fills your body with excitement and dread. How will people respond to this news that is contrary to everything they have ever heard? You tell your family and your friends, but all of them refuse to take their glasses off and look for themselves. "I can clearly see that the sky is red. Have you lost your mind?"; "Someone could hear you saying such things; please keep your voice down--that is forbidden," they respond. This process is infuriating. It is maddening. Why won't they just take their glasses off? Why won't they look for themselves? Perhaps it is because the truth scares them. If the sky is really blue, then that would change the entire dynamic of their lives. They could be rejected by society or--worse--their friends and family. Perhaps they think it is better to hide from the truth, simply not looking at it. It is difficult to break free from a lie told since childhood. Accepting truth takes not only time but also courage.

The topic of baptism is very similar to this imaginary tale. As presented in this book, the Scriptures teach that baptism is for the forgiveness of sins. This revelation is maddening because so many refuse to look, and those who do look explain away the evidence. Will you dare to take your glasses off and examine the sky for yourself? The prospect may be terrifying for you in your given context, but I invite you to take a ride on this quest for truth. Together we will examine the history of baptism [before Christ], the New Testament writings on baptism, the early church's views on baptism, the most common objections today, and, finally, we will discover what to do with this truth. The quest may be scary, but you aren't alone.

(Note: All scriptures used are from the English Standard Version unless otherwise noted.)

ONE

Jewish Baptism Before Christ

There is evidence to suggest that the practice of baptism (immersing someone in water) dates at least as far back as the first century B.C.E. The evidence to support this comes from the findings of what are known as Mikveh. These are dug out pools of water into the ground closely resembling a bathtub. Archaeologists have found hundreds of these all across Jerusalem dating back to the first century B.C.E.[1] Mikveh could easily be mistaken for early bathtubs, but there is other evidence to suggest they were used as a form of ritual washing for Jews. The Jewish practice of immersion still happens today. There are various

---

[1] Ferguson, Baptism in the Early Church: History, Theology, and Liturgy in the First Five Centuries, (Michigan: Eerdmans, 2009) 64.

uses of this immersion, but the most prominent is for Jewish *converts* to be immersed.[2] If things did not change from the first century B.C.E. until today, then that means immersion would have been a practice for conversion. This means once a person decided to convert from some other religion to Judaism they needed to be immersed.

The writings concerning the Jewish practice of immersion are scarce. Judges 12:8-9 seems to imply that a woman was bathing in order to be purified, but this is unclear and bathing didn't necessarily have to mean immersion. Another writing comes from the 3rd century A.D. by Yevamot. He wrote, "Once he has immersed and emerged, he is like a born Jew in every sense."[3] This is stronger evidence and shows that this was the practice as early as the third century after Christ. This along with the vast amount of Mikveh found in Jerusalem is strong evidence that immersion for purification was a common practice before John the Baptist. The practice of Mikveh was not only for conversion, but also for ritual washings such as the priests before entering the Temple, and also before a marriage.

---

[2] Ferguson, Baptism in the Early Church: History, Theology, and Liturgy in the First Five Centuries, 63.
[3] Yevamot 47b, The William Davidson Translation. Website here: https://www.sefaria.org/Yevamot

Another example of baptism before Christ appears with John the Baptist in Mark 1:4-8:

> *John appeared, baptizing in the wilderness and proclaiming a Baptism of repentance for the forgiveness of sin. And all the country of Judea and all Jerusalem were going out to him and were being baptized by him in the river Jordan, confessing their sins......And he preached, saying, "After me comes he who is mightier than I, the strap of whose sandals I am not worthy to stoop down and untie. I have baptized you with water, but he will baptize you with the Holy Spirit.*

John baptized with the purpose of repentance and for the forgiveness of sins. He was pointing the people to Christ. He was preparing the way for the Messiah as was prophesied. John states that while he baptizes with water, this messiah will baptize with the Holy Spirit. The baptism of John and the baptism of Jesus would be two separate baptisms.

John's practice of immersion was not completely shocking to the culture. The practice of the Mikveh meant that Jews had an understanding of what baptism was. For them, hearing "be baptized" meant very simply to be immersed in water. By that token, John's baptism had a spiritual aspect to it; it was not simply a symbol, but was for the forgiveness of the people's sins (Mark 1:4). As we will see, this practice was a temporary forgiveness of sins, and a time was coming in which it would become complete.

Jesus's ministry began at the point in which He himself was baptized by John:

> *Then Jesus came from Galilee to the Jordan to John, to be baptized by him. John would have prevented him, saying, "I need to be baptized by you, and do you come to me?" But Jesus answered him, "Let it be so now, for thus it is fitting for us to fulfill all righteousness." Then he consented. And when Jesus was baptized, immediately he went up from the water, and behold, the heavens were opened to him, and he saw the Spirit of God descending like a dove and coming to rest on him; and behold a voice from heaven said, "This is my beloved Son, with whom I am well pleased (Matthew 3:13-17).*

The Scriptures reveal to us that Jesus was without sin. Despite this, He decided to be baptized to "fulfill all righteousness." It was at the moment when He came out of the water that The Holy Spirit descended upon Him. It was also at this moment that the Father announced Christ as His beloved Son. After being empowered by the Holy Spirit, Jesus thus began His three-year ministry on Earth.

The use of the word "immersion" or "baptism" signified the practice of being immersed in water.[4] Jesus was immersed in water, as the text says, and after He came up out of the water, He received the Spirit. For the practice of the Mikveh, there was also an association with being immersed. The plain understanding of immersion for this culture was to go *into* water. This understanding is significant due to many today charging that immersion in scripture means something other than immersion in water. There are times when this is true (Matthew 3:11), however, due to the practice of immersion with the Mikveh and John the Baptist the most common meaning for this culture when hearing immersion was the practice of being dipped in water. Unless the New Testament specifies that baptism is of The Holy Spirit, Moses, or Fire, then we should understand its default meaning to mean immersion in water.

---

[4] https://www.biblestudytools.com/lexicons/greek/nas/baptizo.html

TWO

The Scriptures on Baptism

N ow let us take a look at the New Testament's passages on baptism. Readers of Scripture come across the word "baptism" and think of one of three things: infant sprinkling, the indwelling of the Holy Spirit, or adult immersion in water. In Greek, the word "baptizo," from which we derive the word "baptism," means "to dip" or "immerse" in water.[5] As we look at each of the following passages, let us consider and determine what type of immersion is being discussed.

> *And He said to them, "Go into all the world and proclaim the gospel to the whole creation. Whoever believes and is baptized will be*

---

[5] https://www.biblestudytools.com/lexicons/greek/nas/bap-tizo.html

9

saved, but whoever does not believe will be condemned (Mark 16:15-16).

Here, we see Jesus telling His disciples that they were to go out into all the world and tell others the Good News. All who hear this Good News, believe it, and are immersed will be saved. When Jesus said this, He was referring to immersion by water. No other reason for baptism had yet been mentioned at this point in the New Testament narrative. The process of being immersed by The Holy Spirit would have been foreign to the apostles at this time. The indwelling presence of the Spirit being poured out on believers did not occur until after Pentecost in Acts 2.

Furthermore, Jesus has two commands listed in conjunction in Mark 16:15-16. He says "believe" *and* "be baptized." Immersion by The Holy Spirit is something only God can do, but being immersed in water is a command humans can obey at their own behest. When Jesus said to "be immersed," this was not a foreign concept to the audience of that day. They had witnessed the Mikveh and how Jews were using it for conversion, and they also had experienced the baptism of John the Baptist. Their first assumption would have been immersion in water as opposed to immersion by The Spirit. The natural reading of the word "immersion" or "baptism" for us should always be "immersion in water" unless otherwise specified.

Other types of immersion were mentioned by John the Baptist, who said "…He will baptize you with the Holy Spirit and fire (Matthew 3:11)." We have now seen three different types of immersion mentioned by Scripture: water immersion; Spirit immersion; and fire immersion. On the day of Pentecost, all three of these came together in perfect harmony (see Acts 2).

In John 14, Jesus tells His disciples that after He leaves them, He will send His Helper. This Helper is a reference to the Comforter or Holy Spirit, as exemplified in John 14:15-17:

> *If you love me, you will keep my commandments. And I will ask the Father, and He will give you another Helper, to be with you forever, even the Spirit of truth, whom the world cannot receive, because it neither sees Him nor knows Him. You know Him, for He dwells with you and will be in you.*

Just after Jesus ascends to be with the Father, we see the story of Pentecost in Acts 2. "Tongues of fire" descended and rested on each of the 12 apostles (Acts 2:2-4). It was not only the tongues that descended on them, but also The Holy Spirit. The Spirit empowered the apostles to speak in foreign languages so that each individual in the audience could understand Peter's message.

When the day of Pentecost arrived, they were all together in one place. And suddenly there came from heaven a sound like a mighty rushing wind, and it filled the entire house where they were sitting. And divided tongues as of fire appeared to them and rested on each one of them. And they were all filled with the Holy Spirit and began to speak in other tongues as the Spirit gave them utterance (Acts 2:1-4).

Later in the chapter, those gathered for Pentecost, Jews from near and far, reacted to the miraculous abilities of the apostles:

"We hear them telling in our own tongues the mighty works of God." And all were amazed and perplexed, saying to one another, "What does this mean?" But others mocking said, "They are filled with new wine" (Acts 2:11b-13).

After the apostles gained the crowd's attention, Peter began his famous first sermon. He tells the Jews that they killed the Messiah. Brokenhearted, the Jews asked (Acts 2:37), "what shall we do?" The next verse tells readers Peter's response.

And Peter said to them, "Repent and be baptized every one of you in the name of Jesus Christ for the forgiveness of your sins, and you will receive the gift of the Holy Spirit'" (Acts 2:38).

Those cut to the heart were told to repent and be immersed in the name of Jesus. After immersion, two things happen. New Christians received the forgiveness of sins, and they received the gift of the Holy Spirit. This type of immersion mentioned in Acts 2 has to be that of being immersed in water; it would simply not make sense for Peter to have meant for them to be "immersed in the Spirit" so that they may receive the gift of the Spirit. Furthermore, as was shown before, one cannot be commanded to be immersed in the Spirit; however, one can be commanded to be immersed in water. Peter was telling this audience to be immersed in water, a concept deeply entrenched in their culture.

The next verse we will examine describes to us in very specific details the purpose of baptism:

Baptism, which corresponds to this, now saves you, not as a removal of dirt from the body but as an appeal to God for a good conscience, through the resurrection of Jesus Christ (I Peter 3:21).

Peter, in this epistle, has just mentioned how baptism corresponds to the flood. The water of the flood cleansed sin from the earth. God did this by destroying all of Creation except for a remnant. Noah was the only man who was found righteous by God. The rest of humanity only had evil in their heart continuously. The waters of the flood cleansed sin then, and, similarly, water now cleanses us from sin today, saving us through obedience to Christ's command. All of this is only possible due to the sacrifice and resurrection of Jesus Christ. Peter tells us the process of immersion doesn't save us because the water washes away the dirt; rather, baptism saves us because it is an appeal to God for a good conscience. It is important to emphasize that there is no power in the water on its own. God has chosen the moment of baptism to be when we are saved from our sins. This salvation is not possible without the work of Christ. This salvation is also not possible without believing in Christ. Baptism is a spiritual act, not merely a physical one as Peter mentions when he says, "not as a removal of dirt". The convert is not saved by taking a bath: they are saved by the washing and regeneration of the Spirit. The mention of the removal of dirt from the flesh is, yet again, an indicator that baptism is an immersion in water. Remember, the natural meaning of immersion is always with water due to the context, history, and prevalence of the practice in the culture.

The next passage we will examine comes from the instructions given to Paul. In Acts 22, Paul had just been beaten by Jews in Jerusalem. Luckily, the Roman guards came to his aid before matters got worse. As Paul was carried away, he asked to speak to the people. That is when he gives a chilling message about his conversion to Christ, perhaps the most poignant of the three accounts in Acts (chapters 9, 22, and 26). He tells how he went to Damascus with the intent to persecute the church, but then he saw a light shining all around him. Falling to the ground, Paul (then Saul) heard a voice saying, *"Saul, Saul, why are you persecuting me?"* This voice was Jesus. The account in Acts 9 reveals that, for 3 days, Paul was blind and did not eat or drink. During these three days, Paul became a believer in Jesus' deity. He had witnessed first-hand the power of Christ, yet as Acts 22:16 iterates, he still needed to do something very essential. This is what he is told after meeting with Ananias, once the three days passed: *"And now why do you wait? Rise and be baptized and wash away your sins, calling on His name"* *(Acts 22:16).*

Ananias asked Paul why he was waiting. Paul needed to rise up and be immersed. This immersion was for the purpose of his sins being washed away. There are many churches all across the globe that need to ask this same question: "Why do you wait?" So many churches/traditions wait months before baptizing their converts. This is often done as a means of baptizing a bunch of people all at once. However, there is *no* biblical example of people waiting before they are baptized. The example from Paul, of him waiting three days to be baptized is actually the longest time a believer waited in the New Testament. Paul only waited this long because he had no other instructions. Ananias was sent by God to speak with Paul, and the moment he got there, he explained to him of the importance of baptism.

The book of Acts has many accounts of conversions for Christians. These conversions mention baptism as happening "within the hour". This was not something postponed or irrelevant to the early church.

Acts 8:12, "But when they believed Philip as he preached good news about the kingdom of God and the name of Jesus Christ, they were baptized, both men and women."

Circumcision, the Jewish requirement for conversion/salvation, was a practice only for men. Baptism, however, extends to all believers. In Acts 16:13-15A, one can see that immersion happened after women and men believed the good news:

And on the Sabbath day we went outside the gate to the riverside, where we supposed there was a place of prayer, and we sat down and spoke to the women who had come together. One who heard us was a woman named Lydia, from the city of Thyatira, a seller of purple goods, who was a worshipper of God. The Lord opened her heart to pay attention to what was said by Paul. And after she was baptized, and her household as well….

Lydia heard the good news about Jesus, and God opened her heart to believe. After she believed, she and her household were baptized. This reference to the household being baptized is a common theme. The assumption is that the entire household believed as well.

Yet another example of baptism for salvation is from Acts 16:25-34. Paul and Silas had just been thrown into a Roman prison. Inside the prison, they prayed and sang praises to God. Suddenly, a great earthquake shook the foundations of the prison freeing both Paul and Silas. The guard over their cells assumes they escaped, and is about to kill himself for fear of a worse fate by his authorities for letting the prisoners escape. Paul calls out with a loud voice and tells the man not to harm himself. The following passage from Acts 16:29-33 tells the rest of the story:

And the jailer called for lights and rushed in, and trembling with fear he fell down before Paul and Silas. Then he brought them out and said, "Sirs, what must I do to be saved?" And they said, "Believe in the Lord Jesus, and you will be saved, you and your household." And they spoke the word of the Lord to him and to all who were in his house. And he took them the same hour of the night and washed their wounds; and he was baptized at once, he and all his family.

Once again, just after belief, at the same hour of the night, this man and his household were baptized. The Scriptures emphasize that he was baptized within the hour for a *reason*. That reason is because baptism is essential, and, as the previous Scriptures showed us, baptism is for the forgiveness of sins. We also can see that this baptism included water as the preceding text says that the jailer was washing their wounds, emphasizing the presence of water.

The next important study comes from Acts 8 with the Ethiopian Eunuch. The Ethiopian Eunuch was traveling to Jerusalem to worship God. This indicates that he was a Jew. As this man was traveling along in his chariot, Philip, a deacon in the early church, was told by the Spirit to join him. When Philip joined the man, he saw that the eunuch was studying from the book of Isaiah. The exact passage the eunuch was studying is a prophecy concerning Jesus. Philip taught the eunuch the Gospel beginning with that Scripture:

> *Then Philip opened his mouth, and beginning with this Scripture he told him the good news about Jesus. And as they were going along the road they came to some water, and the eunuch said, 'See, here is water! What prevents me from being baptized?' And he commanded the chariot to stop, and they both went down into the water, Philip and the eunuch, and he baptized him. And when they came up out of the water, the Spirit of the Lord carried Philip away, and the eunuch saw him no more, and went on his way rejoicing (Acts 8:35-39).*

All the Scripture says that Philip told him was the Good News of Jesus. This means Philip preached to him the Gospel. He shared with him the essential truths of the Christian faith. The eunuch saw for himself that there was water, and he himself took the initiative to be baptized. This means that part of Philip's proclaiming of the Gospel mentioned baptism and its essential nature. The eunuch understood that this needed to be done immediately; furthermore, the Spirit did not carry Philip away until the job was done, after the baptism. If being dipped in water was not vital, then the Spirit would have left after the eunuch first believed. This passage is crucial in the discussion of immersion by water. The eunuch knew that water was included in baptism.

The next important passage for our discussion comes from Paul in his letter to the Romans. Here he is addressing an issue in which the believers at Rome were using the grace they received as an excuse to live in sin.

> *What shall we say then? Are we to continue in sin that grace may abound? By no means! How can we who died to sin still live in it? Do you not know that all of us who have been baptized into Christ Jesus were baptized into his death? We were buried therefore with him by baptism into death, in order that, just as Christ was raised from the dead by the glory of the Father, we too might walk in newness of life (Romans 6:1-6).*

Here, Paul gives further insight into the *meaning and importance* of immersion. Again, this passage clearly reiterates that the natural meaning of baptism in the scriptures is immersion in water. Paul is telling the church of Rome to stop living in sin. He then says, "how can we who have died to sin still live in it?"

Paul proceeds to talk about when the Christians in Rome died to sin. They died to sin when they were dipped in the water. This dipping in water resembles dying and going in the grave, as Christ did. The rising from the water resembles being brought back to life just as Christ was. Thus, being baptized into Jesus Christ means being dipped in the water. The use of the word immersion here does not make sense if Paul was referring to immersion of the Spirit. The practice of being immersed in the water perfectly resembles going into the grave and rising back up again. Paul uses similar language in regard to baptism in *Colossians 2:12*: *"Having been buried with him in baptism, in which you were also raised with him through faith in the powerful working of God, who raised him from the dead."*

Those who have been buried in baptism have also been raised with Christ through faith. The faith in Christ is still necessary during the immersion, and without faith one's dipping in the water is meaningless. This is the powerful working of God. The water does not take away from God's power, but is the means by which He uses His power. Next, let us take a look at what Scripture says concerning being baptized in the name of Christ.

IN THE NAME OF CHRIST

> *"Go therefore and make disciples of all nations,*
> *baptizing them in the name of the Father and*
> *of the Son and of the Holy Spirit" (Matthew*
> *28:19).*

In the above passage, known as the Great Commission, Jesus gave a command. He commanded us to make disciples, baptize them, and to do so in the name of the Father, Son, and Holy Spirit. Jesus connects discipleship with baptism in this passage. A disciple is a follower of Jesus. One cannot be a Christian without following Christ (Luke 9:23). We also see here that it matters in what name a person is baptized. There are different baptisms, and there are different names for those baptisms. The list includes the baptism of Moses, John, Christ, and the Spirit.

> *I baptize you with water for repentance, but*
> *he who is coming after me is mightier than I,*
> *whose sandals I am not worthy to carry. He*
> *will baptize you with the Holy Spirit and fire*
> *(Matthew 3:11).*

From this passage, one can see that John's baptism and Christ's would be fundamentally different. Some take this passage to mean that Jesus' baptism would not include water, but that is not true. The

Ethiopian Eunuch was an undeniable example of a
person learning of Jesus and being immersed in water.
The emphasis here, by John, is that the indwelling of
the Holy Spirit would now occur after baptism, once
Christ came.

> Now a Jew named Apollos, a native of
> Alexandria, came to Ephesus. He was an
> eloquent man, competent in the Scriptures. He
> had been instructed in the way of the Lord.
> And being fervent in spirit, he spoke and
> taught accurately the things concerning Jesus,
> though he knew only the baptism of John. He
> began to speak boldly in the synagogue, but
> when Priscilla and Aquila heard him, they
> took him and explained to him the way of
> God more accurately (Acts 18:24-26).

Apollos was accurate in teaching the story of Jesus,
but he still lacked in something. He only knew of the
baptism of John; however, Priscilla and Aquila took
him aside and taught him the baptism of Jesus. They
told him about the practice of immersion in water, and
also the indwelling of the Spirit that follows baptism.
We can know this is what they taught him due to the
argument just mentioned concerning the Ethiopian
Eunuch. The baptism of John and the baptism of Jesus

both included water. The next form of baptism we will examine also includes water.

For I want you to know, brothers, that our fathers were all under the cloud, and all passed through the sea, and all were baptized into Moses in the cloud and in the sea (1 Corinthians 10:1-2).

The Israelites were baptized into Moses in the sense that they all walked on dry land as the waters of the Red Sea parted around them. They may have walked through completely dry, but in reference to Paul's point there was certainly water involved in this baptism into Moses and the new life after deliverance from Egypt (similarly to how Christians today are delivered from their sins). The cloud in Exodus resembled God's presence among the Israelites. This connection between God's presence and water is seen in the Christian baptism as Jesus teaches in *John 3:5: "Jesus answered, 'Truly, truly, I say to you, unless one is born of water and the Spirit, he cannot enter the kingdom of God.'"*

Some have pointed out that Jesus meant the water surrounding a baby at childbirth. This is a possible interpretation considering the context concerning being born again, but the connection between water and the Spirit is seen throughout the New Testament in reference to immersion, therefore making immersion the most likely meaning of Jesus's words. This passage will be discussed again in Chapter 3: Church History.

The idea of being baptized "in the name of" someone is seen again in Paul's argument to the Corinthians. The Corinthians had divisions among themselves and were arguing, as explained in 1 Corinthians 1:11-17:

> *For it has been reported to me by Chloe's people that there is quarrelling among you, my brothers. What I mean is that each one of you says, "I follow Paul," or "I follow Apollos," or "I follow Cephas," or "I follow Christ." Is Christ divided? Was Paul crucified for you? Or were you baptized in the name of Paul? I thank God that I baptized none of you except Crispus and Gaius, so that no one may say that you were baptized in my name. (I did baptize also the household of Stephanas. Beyond that, I do not know whether I baptized anyone else.) For Christ did not send me to baptize but to preach the gospel, and not with words of eloquent wisdom, lest the cross of Christ be emptied of its power.*

Paul states: "Were you baptized in the name of Paul?" This is a rhetorical question, as all of them had been baptized in the name of Christ. Many have used this passage to state that Paul did not baptize because he did not think it was important. This could not be further from the truth.

I once talked to a missionary who stated that in Africa he never baptizes. His reasoning is that some would get puffed up saying, "I was baptized by the missionary." The result would be that certain converts would think their own baptisms of more importance than others. The temptation would have been even greater for a Christian who was baptized by an apostle! Jesus Himself did not baptize even though He commanded that all be baptized for salvation (Mark 16:16).

Now when Jesus learned that the Pharisees had heard that Jesus was making and baptizing more disciples than John (although Jesus himself did not baptize, but only his disciples), he left Judea and departed again for Galilee (John 4:1-3).

This same Jesus Who didn't baptize *did* order his disciples to go and baptize. When He ordered his disciples to baptize, He was not asking them to immerse people with the Holy Spirit: at that time, He had yet to send His Helper. That would happen after Pentecost. Jesus' command for His disciples to baptize had significance, for, indeed: *"he who believes and is baptized will be saved" (Mark 16:16)*.

We have looked at a great deal of passages that teach quite clearly the importance of immersion. That immersion, as we have studied, is immersion in water. At immersion, we receive the forgiveness of sins, and the gift of the Holy Spirit. We will now take a look at a couple of difficult passages.

DIFFICULT PASSAGES

In Acts 10, Luke describes the moment when the Gentiles (non-Jewish nations) first received the Gospel. The Good News of salvation is offered to all nations from this point, not just Israel. The early church, which was predominantly Jewish, was skeptical at first. They had grown up believing it was unclean to even eat in a Gentile's house; suddenly, they were expected to accept them as brothers and sisters in Christ. It took a special revelation from God to convince Peter to go spread the Gospel to the Gentiles. The end of Acts 10 shows the miraculous result of Peter sharing the Gospel with them.

> *While Peter was still saying these things, the Holy Spirit fell on all who heard the word. And the believers from among the circumcised who had come with Peter were amazed, because*

> the gift of the Holy Spirit was poured out
> even on the Gentiles. For they were hearing
> them speaking in tongues and extolling God.
> Then Peter declared, "Can anyone withhold
> water for baptizing these people, who have
> received the Holy Spirit just as we have?"
> And he commanded them to be baptized in the
> name of Jesus Christ. Then they asked him to
> remain for some days (Acts 10:44-48).

Here, the Gentiles are confirmed by God though the miracle of speaking in tongues. This showed all those present that the Gentiles were, in fact, also the adopted sons and daughters of God. All the people with Peter were amazed at what they witnessed. Peter had already known that the Gentiles were grafted into God's plan, but those with him might not have been so convinced. The Gentiles received the indwelling presence of the Spirit before baptism.

Now, there are many that take from this story the idea that immersion in water is not necessary. They state the we receive the Spirit at belief rather than immersion. This passage would seem to support that view, and perhaps it does tell us something about the way in which God works (see Chapter 5 discussion). But, remember: for Peter and all in attendance this was new! This is the only example of people receiving the Spirit before baptism in the New Testament. This was a special circumstance that God used to confirm, miraculously, that Gentiles can receive the Gospel. Peter then immediately asks if anyone could withhold water for baptizing these people. Again, we see the literal word for water, and this immersion was to take place immediately and without hesitation. They were then baptized in the name of Jesus Christ. We see here again, the norm for describing immersion by water as simply "baptized."

Here is another difficult passage for our discussion revolving around baptism and The Holy Spirit.

> *Now when the apostles at Jerusalem heard that Samaria had received the word of God, they sent to them Peter and John, who came down and prayed for them that they might receive the Holy Spirit, for He had not yet fallen on any of them, but they had only been baptized in the name of the Lord Jesus. Then they laid their hands on them and they received the Holy Spirit (Acts 8:14-17).*

This may seem problematic on the surface, but we must recognize that if the Holy Spirit can only be given to a person through the laying on of hands by the apostles, then no Christian today has the indwelling presence of the Spirit because the apostles have long passed. Furthermore, if no Christian today has the

Spirit, then there are no Christians. To be a saved Christian is to have the indwelling presence of the Spirit (John 3:5). The best way to explain this passage is that the believers in Samaria had not yet received the "full measure" of the Spirit (i.e. the miraculous portion). They had not received the measure of the Spirit which would have given them the ability to perform miracles such as tongues, gifts of healing, and prophecy.

Furthermore, this passage is problematic for those who claim we are saved at the moment of belief, apart from baptism. For them this passage still teaches that the laying on of hands by the apostles is necessary. The plain meaning of the text is frequently not the correct interpretation. This is because we often interpret with 21st century lens rather than 1st century lens. This passage is a great example of the need to dive deep in our interpretation of Scripture. Looking more closely, we see that the people in Samaria followed a formula, or sequence, of obedience in order to obtain salvation. We see the same formula for new converts from Paul in Ephesus in Acts 19. The sequence was as follows: belief in the Gospel, baptism in water in the name of Jesus Christ, and laying on of hands by the apostle(s) for the full measure of the Spirit (i.e. receiving miraculous gifts).

And it happened that while Apollos was at Corinth, Paul passed through the inland country and came to Ephesus. There he found some disciples. And he said to them, "Did you receive the Holy Spirit when you believed?" And they said, "No, we have not even heard that there is a Holy Spirit." And he said, "Into what then were you baptized?" They said, "Into John's baptism." And Paul said, "John baptized with the baptism of repentance, telling the people to believe in the one who was to come after him, that is, Jesus." On hearing this, they were baptized in the name of the Lord Jesus. And when Paul had laid his hands on them, the Holy Spirit came on them, and they began speaking in tongues and prophesying (Acts 19:1-6).

The believers in Ephesus had only been baptized in the name of John. John's baptism, as was discussed earlier, differed from Jesus', but water was still used in Christ's baptism. Here, Paul baptized them in the name of Jesus. After immersing them he laid his hands on them. One of the key differences in John's baptism and Christ's was that Jesus' baptism included the indwelling presence of the Spirit. This text is another example of the believers not receiving the miraculous portion of the Spirit until the laying on of hands. This is speaking of the full measure of the Spirit resulting in miracles, not the indwelling presence received at baptism.

In conclusion, after looking at what Scripture says on this topic, one would be hard-pressed to deny that immersion in water is for the forgiveness of sins. There are still certain preconceptions with which people come to the text; these cause them to reject that baptism leads to regeneration through faith. These preconceptions will be considered in Chapter 4. Now, we must examine what the early church believed on this matter, that being the Christians who came immediately after the New Testament.

THREE

Church History on Baptism

T his section will examine the first three centuries of church history after Christ. Church history is important for us because we can see what the traditional interpretations were by the early church. That is, if Scripture is clear on a particular subject, and the early church fathers agreed with that interpretation, then it is safe to say that this study will be case-closed. Let me be clear in stating that the early church fathers are not inspired. If we followed everything they *believed*, then our practices would be a mess. The church fathers often contradict each other; history tells us they had beliefs which would be unusual to us, such as baptizing people naked or dipping them in the water three times. The point is not that we follow everything they say, but that we can learn from them on this topic.

It is important to look at two passages in Scripture that the early church fathers often quoted in their view of baptism. These passages alone do not lead to a "regeneration" view of baptism, but when read in light of the passages in the last sections, it is plain to see that the writer was referring to baptism, or that God can use water as a means of healing.

> *He saved us, not because of works done by us in righteousness, but according to his own mercy, by the washing of regeneration and renewal of the Holy Spirit (Titus 3:5).*

One could easily state that this passage is simply using the term "washing" symbolically to refer to how God cleanses believers from their sins. This is true, but in light of the previously quoted verses, it is also true that this cleansing of sins happens at baptism. This washing in the water is the same moment that the Holy Spirit indwells a person (Acts 2:38). This passage was applied to baptism time and time again by several church fathers throughout the first 3 centuries of the church's existence.

2 Kings 5 tells the story of Naaman. Naaman was a commander of the army of the king of Syria. He was a man of valor, but he was also a leper. Leprosy is a terrible skin disease that resulted in a person being cast off from society, lest he spread it to others. Naaman

heard that a prophet in Israel could heal him of his leprosy. Thus, he went to Israel and stood in front of the prophet Elisha's house. There, Elisha's servant brought a message to Naaman:

> *"Go and wash in the Jordan seven times, and your flesh shall be restored, and you shall be clean." But Naaman was angry and went away, saying, "Behold, I thought that he would surely come out to me and stand and call upon the name of the Lord his God, and wave his hand over the place and cure the leper. Are not Abana and Pharpar, the rivers of Damascus, better than all the waters of Israel? Could I not wash in them and be clean?" So he turned and went away in rage. But his servants came near and said to him, "My father, it is a great word the prophet has spoken to you; will you not do it? Has he actually said to you, 'Wash and be clean'?" So he went down and dipped himself seven times in the Jordan, according to the word of the man of God, and his flesh was restored like the flesh of a little child, and he was clean (2 Kings 5:10b-14).*

Church fathers alluded to this passage to show that, just as Namaan was cleansed through water, so also is the Christian cleansed and regenerated through water. This is similar to Paul claiming that, just as Israel was baptized through the Red Sea, so also are Christians now baptized (1 Corinthians 10:1-2).

The next portion of this section shall focus on the historical texts used to talk about baptism in the early church. The first quote comes from the Epistle of Barnabas. This text was written in the second century:

> This He saith, because we go down into the water laden with sins and filth, and rise up from it bearing fruit in the heart, resting our fear and hope on Jesus in the spirit... (Barnabas 11:11)[6]

Barnabas states that one goes into the water with his or her uncleanness and sins intact. This is to say that the forgiveness of sins is not given to a person at the point of belief, but he carries them even to the point of baptism, which the New Testament teaches.

The next quote comes from Herma in his writing, *The Shepherd*. This work dates back to second century Rome[7]:

---

[6] The Epistle of Barnabas, Translated by J.B. Lightfoot, **http://www.earlychristianwritings.com/text/barnabas-lightfoot.html**. (Ferguson, 210).

[7] Ferguson, Baptism in the Early Church: History, Theology, and Liturgy in the First Five Centuries, 214.

"...I have heard, Sir," say I, "from certain teachers that there is no other repentance, save that which took place when we went down into the water and obtained remission of our former sins." He said to me; "Thou hast well heard; for so it is." (Mandates 4.3.31.1-2)[8]

The above passage inundates that one went down into the water to receive the forgiveness of sins. Another writing from Herma states:

"They were obliged," he answered, "to ascend through water in order that they may be made alive... The seal then is the water: They descend into the water dead, and they arise alive. And to them, accordingly, was this seal preached, and they made use of it that they might enter into the kingdom of God." (Similitudes 9.16)[9]

---

[8] The Shepherd of Hermas, Mandates 4.3.31.1-2, Translated by J.B. Lightfoot, **http://www.earlychristianwritings.com/ text/shepherd-lightfoot.html**. (Ferguson, 216).
[9] The Shepherd of Hermas, Similitudes 9.16, Translated by J.B. Lightfoot, **https://rfwma.org/wp-content/up- loads/2019/04/Shepherd-of-Hermas-Similitudes.pdf** (Ferguson, 217).

The belief here is that a person is made alive after they come up out of the water. This is very similar to Paul's statement that baptism unites believers into a death like Christ's (Romans 6:5). Coming up out of the water makes one alive or born again (John 3:5). There is also reference that this leads to one entering the kingdom of God, which is also seen in John 3:5. The seal in the water can be attributed to 2 Corinthians 1:22: *"And who has also put his seal on us and given us his Spirit in our hearts as a guarantee"*. This one passage is loaded with scripture and references from the New Testament, all giving the indication that immersion of water leads to salvation.

The next historical passage of interest was written by Justin Martyr. He was martyred for his beliefs circa 165 A.D., and his work, *1 Apology,* was around 150:

> Then they are led by us to where there is water, and in the manner of the regeneration by which we ourselves were regenerated they are regenerated. For at the time they are washed in the water in the name of God the Master and Father of all, and of our Savior Jesus Christ, and of the Holy Spirit. For Christ also said, "Unless you are regenerated you cannot

enter into the kingdom of heaven." (1 Apology 61:1-4)[10]

Justin Martyr specifies the process of baptism as practiced by the early church. He states that the elder Christians led new converts to water. They then dipped them into the water for regeneration. Regeneration simply means being made new in Christ, receiving forgiveness of sins, and receiving the gift of the Holy Spirit. He then states that they were "washed" in the water. This is a reference to *Titus 3:5, "….the washing of regeneration and renewal of the Holy Spirit."* Martyr clarifies that the washing of regeneration (immersion in the waters of baptism) in Titus 3:5 is the process by which God saves His children. Martyr then quotes Jesus, saying, "unless you are regenerated you cannot enter into the kingdom of heaven." This quote does not exist in Scripture verbatim, but the church fathers frequently cited another passage, analogous to Martyr's statement, when speaking of baptism. This verse is *John 3:5: "Jesus answered, 'Truly, truly, I say to you, unless one is born of water and the Spirit, he cannot enter the kingdom of God.'"* In Chapter 2, recall how some interpret (falsely) water in this verse to mean the water released during childbirth. For Martyr, however, the correct interpretation was that one must be born again

---

[10] Ferguson, Baptism in the Early Church: History, Theology, and Liturgy in the First Five Centuries, 237.

through the process of baptism, and then they will also receive the gift of the Spirit.

Theophilus of Antioch wrote *To Autolycus* in about 180.[11] In this work, he states:

> On the fifth day the living creatures which proceed from the waters were produced, through which also is revealed the manifold wisdom of God in these things; for who could count their multitude and very various kinds? Moreover, the things proceeding from the waters were blessed by God, that his also might be a sign of men's being destined to receive repentance and remission of sins, through the water and laver of regerneration – as many come to the truth, and are born again, and receive blessing from God. (*To Autolycus* 2.16)[12]

Here, again, a source as early as 180 A.D. is speaking of the forgiveness of sins through water. The water is

---

[11] Ferguson, Baptism in the Early Church: History, Theology, and Liturgy in the First Five Centuries, 246.

[12] Theophilus, To Autolycus, translation by Marcus Dods, **https://www.newadvent.org/fathers/02041.htm**. (Ferguson, 303).

connected to regeneration (Titus 3:5) as well as to being born again (John 3:5).

The next source comes from Irenaeus, who also wrote in the second century. He was a literary opponent of the Gnostics of his day.[13] He opposed false doctrine and many of his statements have been preserved regarding baptism:

> First of all, [it] admonishes us to remember that we have received baptism for remission of sins in the name of God the Father, and in the name of Jesus Christ, the Son of God, who became incarnate and died and was raised, and in the Holy Spirit of God.[14]

This quote from Irenaeus ties "the remission of sins" directly to baptism; this is similar to Acts 2:38:

> [Scripture] says, "And he [Naaman] baptized himself in the Jordan seven times." It was not in vain that Naaman the leper of old, when he was baptized,

---

[13] Ferguson, Baptism in the Early Church: History, Theology, and Liturgy in the First Five Centuries, 303.

[14] *Demonstration 3* (Smith, p.49). Demonstration 3, translation by Joseph P. Smith, St. Irenaeus: Proof of the Apostolic Preaching, Ancient Christian Writers 16 (New York: Newman [Paulist], 1952, P.49. (Ferguson, 304).

was cleansed, but it was a sign to us. We
who are lepers in our sins are cleansed
from our old transgressions through the
holy water and the invocation of the
Lord.[15]

One may draw several conclusions from this passage.
Firstly, the natural means of baptism was immersion in
water. Unless otherwise specified, one should assume
baptism in the Scriptures refers to water immersion.
Secondly, Irenaeus is using an Old Testament text
to show God using the water for cleansing. Thirdly,
Christians are cleansed from their old transgressions
at baptism. Irenaeus affirms Acts 2:38, repeating that
the Holy Spirit is given to Christians at baptism. In
Irenaeus' words, "...when there abides constantly
in them the Holy Spirit, who is given by Him in
baptism." [16]

Another prominent member of the early church,
Clement of Alexandria, states, "The Lord invites to
the bath, to salvation, to enlightenment."[17] The "bath"
here is a frequent term in ancient history for baptism.
He ties together the idea of this "bath" to salvation.

---

[15] Irenaeus, Fragment 34 (W. W. Harvey, Sancti Irenaei Libros
quinque adversus haereses [Cambridge, 1857; repr. Ridgewood,
NJ: Gregg, 1965], #33). (Ferguson, 305).

[16] *Demonstration 42* (Smith, p.74) (Ferguson, 305).

[17] *Exhortation* 10.94.2. (Ferguson, 309).

In another quote, Clement affirms his poignant view of baptism, saying: "Transgressions are forgiven... by the baptism that pertains to the Word. We thoroughly wash all sins away from ourselves and at once are no longer evil."[18] [19]

The following sources all come from the third century. According to the historian, Hippolytus, there was a practice established where "catechumens" were to be taught God's Word for three years before they could be baptized.[20] This seems to be a new development in the third century. "Catechumens" were not considered Christians. They were on the way to becoming Christians, but they needed to be properly taught. These catechumens were given assurances concerning their own salvation in case a tragedy happened before they were baptized. In this case, it is stated by Hippolytus that the catechumen will be justified because he would have received baptism in his own blood.[21] This practice of waiting for three years springs up purely from tradition and is not the Biblical view. The New Testament always

---

[18] Ferguson, Baptism in the Early Church: History, Theology, and Liturgy in the First Five Centuries, 312.

[19] *Instructor* 1.6.50.4 (Ferguson, 312).

[20] Ferguson, Baptism in the Early Church: History, Theology, and Liturgy in the First Five Centuries, 329.

[21] Ferguson, Baptism in the Early Church: History, Theology, and Liturgy in the First Five Centuries, 329.

attests to an immediate baptism after hearing the word of God (Acts 22:16). It is worth noting, however, that a high view of baptism (for the forgiveness of sins) is still maintained three centuries after Christ.

The next source in the third century comes from Tertullian. He is one of the first theologians, writing about church history, to address the belief of baptism not being necessary for salvation. He did not believe this, but he wrote against these "most villainous" persons who attribute faith alone as able to save.[22] Tertullian actually argues against many of the same arguments that arise today in the discussion of baptism. He explained that, "when Paul had believed he was then baptized," quoting Acts 22:16 (see Chapter 2).[23] He addressed Paul's claim in 1 Cor. 1:17 that he did not come to baptize, but to preach the Gospel. Tertullian's response was, "Preaching comes first, baptizing later, when preaching has preceded."[24]

Cyprian of Carthage also wrote in the third century:

> All who arrive at the divine bath by the sanctification of baptism, put off the old self be the grace of the saving laver, and, renewed by the Holy Spirit from the filth

---

[22] Tertullian, Baptism 13.1 (Ferguson, 339).
[23] Tertullian, Baptism 13.4 (Ferguson, 339).
[24] Tertullian, Baptism 14.2 (Ferguson, 340).

of the old contagion, are purged by a second birth.(Dress of Virgins, 23.) [25]

Cyprian stated that people put off their old selves at baptism. This is seen in Ephesians 4:22, in which Paul told the Ephesians to put off their old selves. Cyprian, at the very least, was using the same language as Paul here. Cyprian emphasized the Holy Spirit's role in baptism. In another writing he stated: "Water by itself cannot cleanse sins and sanctify a person unless it possesses the Holy Spirit as well". (Letters, 74)[26] This is a healthy view of baptism, as it attributes the saving power to God rather than the water. Nevertheless, the water is still the place and means by which The Spirit saves through faith in Christ.

Origen wrote in the third century concerning baptism, but also recorded the early development of infant baptism in the young church. In this passage he is giving a defense as to why children need to be baptized:

> Christian brethren often ask a question. The passage from Scripture read today encourages me to treat it again. Little children are baptized "for the remission of sins." Whose sins are they? When did

---

[25] Cyprian of Carthage, *Dress of Virgins*, 23. (Ferguson, 358).
[26] Cyprian of Carthage, Letters, 74. (Ferguson, *359*).

they sin? Or how can this explanation of the baptismal washing be maintained in the case of small children, except according to the interpretation we spoke of a little earlier? "No man is clean of stain, not even if his life upon the earth had lasted but a single day" [Job 14:4-5]. Through the mystery of baptism, the stains of birth are put aside. For this reason, even small children are baptized. For "Unless born of water and the Spirit one cannot enter the kingdom of heaven." (*Homilies on Luke* 14.5 on Luke 2:22)[27]

This passage from Origen reveals that, even in this flawed perspective, the view was still held that baptism was essential for the forgiveness of sins. It is harmful, however, to assume the need for baptism must take place even among children or infants. Again, this was not the Biblical view in the first century and seems to have gradually creeped into various church settings in the third century. Infant baptism did not become the norm until the late fourth century.[28]

---

[27] Joseph T. Lienhard, *Origen: Homilies on Luke*, Fragments on Luke, Fathers of the Church 94 (Washington: Catholic University of America Press, 1996). (Ferguson, 367).

[28] Ferguson, Baptism in the Early Church: History, Theology, and Liturgy in the First Five Centuries, 379.

Origen, furthermore, connected two Old Testament passages to the Christian baptism:

> "Thus it is fitting, after the parting of the Red Sea, that is, after the grace of baptism, for the carnal vices of our old habits to be removed from us by means of our Lord Jesus, so that we can be free from the Egyptian reproaches [Josh. 5.9].[29]"

Origen connected the Christian baptism to the baptism of Moses by which the Israelites were "under the Red Sea." This "baptism of Moses" led to their salvation from the bondage of the Egyptians. The connection would be the Christian baptism rescuing humans from the bondage of sin. Another reference to the Old Testament concerning baptism:

> Men covered with the filth of leprosy are cleansed in the mystery of baptism by the spiritual Elijah, our Lord and Savior. To you he says, "Get up and go into the Jordan and wash, and your flesh will be restored to you' [2 Kings 5:10]....

---

[29] Translation by Barbara J. Bruce, Origen: Homiles on Joshua, Fathers of the Church 105 (Washington: Catholic University of America Press, 2002), p. 216. (Ferguson, 402).

> When [Naaman] washed, he fulfilled the mystery of baptism, 'and his flesh became like the flesh of a child." Which child? The one that is born "in the washing of rebirth" [regeneration – Tit. 3:5] in Christ Jesus. (33.5)[30]

Origen was connecting the idea of a 'spiritual Elijah' to Jesus. He recalled the story of Naaman being cleansed from his leprosy in the Jordan. Just as God used water at this time to cleanse the flesh, he now uses the water of baptism to cleanse the soul.

The evidence that water was used in baptism for the remission of sins is overwhelming when considering church history. While history is not needed to have a Biblical view of baptism, it certainly provides adequate evidence to the way the early church applied the Scriptures. Those who reject water baptism as essential have an entire mountain of historical and Biblical evidence to surpass.

---

[30] Translation by Joseph T. Lienhard, Origen: Homilies on Luke, Fragments on Luke, Fathers of the Church 94 (Washington: Catholic University of America Press, 1996), p. 136. (Ferguson, 404).

FOUR

Objections

M any have presented objections when it comes to the topic of baptism. It is likely that several reading up to this point have seen the evidence just presented, but are still unable to accept it. There is a mountain of tradition which must be surpassed in order to accept baptism as essential. This mountain of tradition takes the form of sermons in which baptism is never mentioned but only faith. It comes in cynical whispers such as, "I can't believe Fred believes baptism is essential." It comes from parents or grandparents who would be devastated if their child veered from the traditions in which they were brought up. As we consider many of the objections towards baptism, I challenge you to set aside your preconceived notions.

The first objection falls under the umbrella of what

might be called "explaining away the text." There are many whose approach to the reading of baptism involves imaginative attempts to explain away what the text is clearly saying. There are times when the "clear meaning" of the text is not the accurate meaning of the text, but that mostly involves the error of our own filter when reading. Remember, we are 2,000 years removed from the text, and that makes interpretation difficult at times. It is also the case that sometimes we do not accept the "clear meaning" of a passage because that text seems to be presenting a doctrine that the rest of Scripture contradicts. It is a completely different case when discussing baptism, however, because the evidence is overwhelming. Albeit, we shall look at a few common examples of "explaining away the text" as it relates to baptism.

In Acts 22:16, Paul is instructed to, *"Rise and be baptized and wash away your sins, 'calling on his name.'"* The clear meaning of this text is that, at baptism, God washes away one's sins. There is also a reference to 'calling on his name.' In the book *Understanding Four Views on Baptism,* the scholar Thomas J. Nettles writes this concerning our passage:

> Does this mean that in baptism Paul was
> to consider his sins as being washed away?
> The text does not support this viewpoint.
> His baptism identifies him with the Jesus

whom he recently persecuted and whose mission was defined in terms of his submission to the baptism of John. The washing away of sins is connected with calling on Jesus' name. The participle should be considered instrumental: "by calling on his name." This phrase duplicates Peter's use of the same verse in Joel in the sermon at Pentecost (Acts 2:21). Paul uses it in Romans 10:13: "Everyone who calls on the name of the Lord will be saved." There he shows that such calling is the mouth's expression of the heart's conviction that salvation depends on the atoning work of Christ verified as acceptable by the resurrection. At his conversion, therefore, Paul expressed his persuasion that Jesus was Lord and Christ and that the resurrection represented the culmination of Christ's atoning work. In his heart- in the seat of his moral judgment and affections- he knew that Christ's death was necessary for salvation.[31]

---

[31] John H. Armstrong, *Understanding Four Views on Baptism*, (Michigan: Zondervan, 2007), 46.

The claim here by Thomas J. Nettles is that the washing away of Paul's sins was connected to him calling on the name of the Lord in a confession, rather than the baptism of Acts 22:16. A clear reading of the text would deny this interpretation. The phrase "wash your sins away" has clear implications to the washing presented in water at baptism. The supporting passages Nettles quotes actually support that baptism is for regeneration, though he intended to use them to deny it. This phrase "calling on the name of the Lord" finds its roots in Joel 2. This is the same passage that Peter included in his sermon at Pentecost. At the end of Peter's speech he connected the coming of the Holy Spirit, and the calling on the name of the Lord, to baptism by declaring, in *Acts 2:38, "Repent and be baptized everyone one of you in the name of Jesus Christ for the forgiveness of your sins, and you will receive the gift of the Holy Spirit."* The idea of "calling on the name of the Lord," though it dated back to Joel, was used in connection to baptism in both Acts 2:38 and Acts 22:16.

Nettles presents another argument in the above quote where he "explains away the text." In 2 Peter 3:21 Peter says, *"Baptism... now saves you, not as a removal of dirt from the body but as an appeal to God for a good conscience..."* In response to this passage, Nettles states, "The text says that baptism does not remove the moral filth natural to life in this body."[32] Nettle's argument is that baptism does not cleanse of sins or moral "filth," but Peter did not mention anything about moral filth as Nettle is trying to claim. Peter's argument is actually quite natural. The washing in water at baptism is not for the purpose of removing dirt from one's body, such as in a bath, but, instead, baptism has an effect on one at a spiritual level. Baptism saves through the power of Jesus Christ. This interpretation of 2 Peter 3:21 is more logical, and more congruent with Peter's sermon at Pentecost.

Another common "explaining away" of the text happens with Acts 2:38. It has often been the claim that the word "for" actually means "because of." Acts 2:38 is then read as ".. Repent and be baptized every one of you in the name of Jesus Christ because of the forgiveness of your sins.." The argument thus follows that a person is baptized *because* of the forgiveness of sins they had already received at the time of belief. There are several problems with this interpretation, however. Firstly, the Greek word "eis" which is "for" in this text is found in other places of Scripture where it means "into," "unto," and "towards." According to the *Exegetical Dictionary of the New Testament*, the word is "an indicator of direction toward a goal."[33]

---

[32] John H. Armstrong, *Understanding Four Views on Baptism*, 46.
[33] Balz, Horst and Gerhard Schneider. Exegetical Dictionary of the New Testament, Vol 1, (Michigan: Eerdmans, 1978), 398.

An example of this is in *Matthew 26:28: "for this is my blood of the covenant, which is poured out for many for the forgiveness of sins."* The same Greek word "eis" is found in this passage as well, yet no one would dare claim that Jesus's blood is "because of" the forgiveness of sins. In English, the word "for" can sometimes also mean "because of." An example of this would be, "Mark went to the hospital for his heart attack." The heart attack has already taken place, and he is going to the hospital *because* of this condition. Greek is different from English, however, and the "eis" version of "for" always means "into, unto, and towards." Secondly, this would mean also that repentance is because of the forgiveness of sins, but that would contradict much of Scripture such as Acts 3:19, *"Repent therefore, and turn again, that your sins may be blotted out.."* Acts 2:38 tells us that both baptism and repentance is "for/towards" the forgiveness of sins, not because of the forgiveness of sins. Thirdly, the English translators could have easily translated this as "because of," but that would have been improper. Instead they unanimously translate the word "for" because baptism leads one towards the forgiveness of sins. It is worth noting that even if someone interprets this word as "because of" this would still leave a great many New Testament passages needing to be explained away as well.

Another passage with which people often explain away is *Mark 16:16: "Whoever believes and is baptized will be saved, but whoever does not believe will be condemned.*" It is often stated that the text nowhere states that those who are not baptized will be condemned it only states those who do not believe are condemned. This is true, but Jesus did not need to claim that those who are not baptized will be condemned because the natural sequence is for a person to believe first and then be baptized. If a person does not believe, then they naturally will not be baptized. Jesus has plainly stated what must be done to be saved, belief *and* baptism; they are conjunctive. If a person was told that if they drive to the store and buy a piece of candy, they will receive a million dollars, then would they dare only drive to the store?

The next "explaining away of the text" comes from Galatians 3:27, which states: *"For as many of you as were baptized into Christ have put on Christ."* To put on Christ is to be added to the church, and the church only consists of those who are saved. Concerning this passage John H. Armstrong states:

> How strange would it be that Paul introduces a new ceremony by which Christ's saving work becomes effectual? Could he really be saying, "Reject the heretical formula of hearing plus believing plus circumcision; instead replace it with hearing plus believing plus baptism?"

That interpretation of baptism would run counter to Paul's purpose in Galatians.[34]

Armstrong's argument is based off the idea that Paul is rejecting all ceremonies in Galatians. This is, simply, false. Yes, Galatians is a letter about Christian Jews needing to move on from the Old Law of Moses. They were Christians now under a new covenant. Naturally, as should be expected, they struggled to remove all of the traditions from their youth, such as circumcision, which was essential to becoming a Jew. Paul is telling them to move on. Paul is not referring to the New Covenant and baptism; he is speaking on the Old Covenant and circumcision. Armstrong states that it would be strange for Paul to introduce a new ceremony for Christ's saving work to become effectual, but Paul is not introducing a new ceremony. This ceremony was installed by Christ (Mark 16:16) and was the very same instructions by which Paul was told to be saved (Acts 22:16). For Paul, in Galatians and his other letters, baptism was essential.

Another "explaining away of the text" is found in Colossians 2:11–12 which reads:

> *In him also you were circumcised with a circumcision made without hands, by putting off the body of the flesh, by the circumcision*

---

[34] John H. Armstrong, *Understanding Four Views on Baptism*, 48.

of Christ, having been buried with him in baptism, in which you were also raised with him through faith in the powerful working of God, who raised him from the dead.

It is at baptism that one is united into Christ's death. This is significant because Paul tells us this in his letter to Rome:

Do you not know that all of us have been baptized into Christ Jesus were baptized into his death? We were buried therefore with him by baptism into death, in order that, just as Christ was raised from the dead by the glory of the Father, we too might walk in newness of life. For if we have been united with him in a death like his, we shall certainly be untied with him in a resurrection like his (Romans 6:3-5).

It is at baptism that we die to our old self and come up out of the waters a new creation, clothed with Christ. Paul finds the death found in baptism to be salvific. If we have been united into Christ's death, then we will certainly be raised up and resurrected as He was. This understanding is of crucial importance as we examine John Piper's "explaining away of the text" in Colossians 2:11-12. Piper states:

You were buried with him and raised
with him in baptism *through faith*. The
burial with Christ in the water and the
rising with Christ out of the water, it
seems to me from that text, are not what
unites us to Christ – that is, the going
under the water, the coming up out of
the water. That's not what unites you
to Christ. It is *through faith* that you are
decisively united to Christ.[35]

Piper is trying to claim that, because Paul states
in Colossians 2:11-12 that we are "raised with him
through faith," that he meant baptism is separated from
the action. Piper states that, "it is through faith that
you are decisively united to Christ." Why then does
Paul mention specifically baptism in Colossians and
Romans as uniting us to Christ's death? Paul's entire
point is to describe how baptism unites us to Christ,
and he states that this is done "through faith." The
central saving component for the human is 'faith in
Christ.' We are saved *through* faith in Christ *at* baptism.
That is Paul's message and what he was trying to
convey. For the person who is baptized without faith
it is meaningless.

---

[35] https://www.desiringgod.org/interviews/is-baptism-nec-
essary-for salvation?fbclid=IwAR2GpP522pKhFYZbZm13b-
ZWZN3kMm71QusvbSCyzgyzBeZZuq9jcttKLUeI

We will now take a look at the objection that faith alone saves and not baptism. This objection is built on the passages in Scripture which seem to imply we are saved at the point of belief. To begin, we will resume Piper's argument.

Piper continues his argument with a strong passage. He cites Romans 4:11 which reads:

> *He received the sign of circumcision as a seal of the righteousness that he had by faith while he was still uncircumcised. The purpose was to make him the father of all who believe without being circumcised, so that righteousness would be counted to them as well.*

Piper emphasizes how Abraham was given the sign of circumcision which represented his saving faith. His point is that Abraham was counted righteous by God before his circumcision; therefore, the Christian is saved by faith before baptism. This is a strong argument. The only problem is that Paul never asserts that baptism is the new circumcision. Paul's purpose in this passage is to show that man is saved by faith apart from the Old Law (we are now under the New Law), and even Abraham (who lived before the Old Law) was justified before his circumcision. The Christian is still saved by faith, but what exactly does Paul mean when he says that? This question is at the heart of the discussion here.

We must now dive into a deep theological discussion so that our next common objection can be presented. There is a tension in the Scriptures between faith and works. This tension is neither easy to unscramble nor understand. Speaking of this, Paul states in *1 Cor. 13:12: "For now we see in a mirror dimly, but then face to face. Now I know in part; then I shall know fully, even as I have been fully known."* What we know of God and His plan is seen, but it is seen darkly. The Way is not always crystal clear; in fact, it is often difficult to understand certain Scriptures. Peter himself says this in 2 Peter 3:16 when referring to Paul's writings: *"As he does in all his letters when he speaks in them of these matters. There are some things in them that are hard to understand, which the ignorant and unstable twist to their own destruction, as they do the other Scriptures".* We must be both careful and humble when speaking on salvation matters. Let us begin.

> *For by grace you have been saved through faith. And this is not your own doing; it is the gift of God, not a result of works, so that no one may boast. For we are his workmanship, created in Christ Jesus for good works, which God prepared beforehand, that we should walk in them. (Ephesians 2:8-10)*

Paul has just stated a couple of important matters for us to consider. Firstly, our salvation is through faith. We do not earn our salvation. It is completely independent of any amount of good works we could do. Secondly, we are created in Christ Jesus for good works. The implication is that those who are saved *will* walk in good works. We are not saved by good works, but the saved will walk in them.

Another significant passage for this discussion is *Philippians 2:12-13:*

> *Therefore, my beloved, as you have always obeyed, so now, not only as in my presence but much more in my absence, work out your own salvation with fear and trembling, for it is God who works in you, both to will and to work for his good pleasure.*

The implication from this passage is that we must "work out our own salvation." Is this contradictory to what Paul just claimed? Is salvation still possible apart from works? No. The difference is that we are justified and cleansed from sins based solely on faith alone, rather than good works. This faith which saves us then *empowers us* for good works, which God aids us in doing. The Christian must, however, make a conscious decision to "work out their own salvation." This means we must deliberately be striving to walk with Christ. Abraham was justified by his faith before circumcision, but he was still circumcised. This would have been an unbelievably painful and hard decision/work for Abraham to follow. My argument is that, while we are justified through faith, not works, we are still held accountable by God to follow Him. Christians who turn their back on the faith and choose a path contrary to Christ are no longer saved. God expects us to follow Him.

James 2:14-26 is an entire passage dedicated to showing the importance of works alongside faith. James even says this concerning Abraham in verse 21, *"Was not Abraham our father justified by works when he offered up his son Isaac on the altar?"* The answer to James's rhetorical question is "Yes, Abraham was justified by works!" My approach to this difficult tension between faith and works is simply this: we are saved and made a New Creation by our faith, but the ongoing process of being saved requires that we walk with Christ. And, He aids us in doing this. This topic is approaching deep theological issues and territory that is beyond the scope of this book. This is all relevant, however, due to the objection that baptism is a work and thus cannot be essential.

Baptism is not a work, at least not the same type of work as that about which Paul spoke earlier. Baptism involves being dipped in water by another person after a person has made an intellectual assent, confessing that Christ is the Son of God. After this, he or she has made the conscious decision to follow Jesus. Those who claim baptism is a work and cannot be essential are often the same ones who claim a person must confess Christ before others to be saved. Is confession not a work also? Technically, it is a work, but this is certainly not the kind of work Paul had in mind. *Matthew 10:32-33 states: "So everyone who acknowledges me before men, I also will acknowledge before my Father who is in heaven, but whoever denies me before men, I also will deny before my Father who is in heaven".* Confession is essential for the Christian. Even for those who deny that confession is essential it is still illogical to call baptism a work, but then not admit that coming to an "intellectual assent" (that being choosing in your mind that Christ is the Son of God) is a work. A person must still choose to believe in Christ and to follow Him. Both of these general actions constitute "work."

When approaching Scripture, and namely a select number of passages in which Paul discusses being saved by faith and works, it is important that we distinguish which type of works Paul had in mind. Many would like to claim that Paul was referring to "all" works, but to make such an assertion is to make Paul contradict himself. Furthermore, inspired writers such as Paul and James would contradict each other, causing the infallible Scriptures to be at odds. There are three types of works to which Paul could be referring. Firstly, he could be referring to works of the Old Law. In other words, he was stating that people are saved by faith rather than circumcision! This is extremely relevant because Paul was often refuting ideas such as "you must still be circumcised" among Judaizing Christians; in fact, much of Galatians centers on this topic of Old Law vs. the Law of Christ. Secondly, Paul could be referring to works of a moral nature. These include feeding the poor, preaching the gospel, and eschewing sinful practices. Third, Paul could be speaking of works which lead to salvation. These include faith, repentance, confession, and baptism. Paul is never referring to the latter when he claims we are saved by faith not by works. It is important that we recognize the different uses of "work" to which Paul could be referring. Failure to recognize this results in claiming that Paul believed all works were excluded from salvation, and that cannot be the case.

When Paul states that we are saved by faith, he is using the term "faith" to refer to all that constitutes becoming a Christian. The word faith is used as an "umbrella term," meaning it resembles all that comes with it. Living in Tennessee, I grew up using the term "Coke" a lot. This was not because I was especially fond of Coca-Cola. Rather, we tend to use "Coke" as an umbrella term for all sorts of soft drinks. Technically speaking, the word "Coke," though it is short for Coca-Cola, can be used in reference to Mountain-Dew, Dr. Pepper, Fanta, and many more carbonated beverages. When Paul says we are saved by faith, he is using the term to describe the steps it takes to become a Christian, as opposed to the mere earning of salvation. Paul is not a stranger to the idea that moral works matter at Judgement. Only three chapters after Paul declares that we are "saved by grace through faith," he states: *"For you may be sure of this, that everyone who is sexually immoral or impure, or who is covetous (that is, an idolater), has no inheritance in the kingdom of Christ and God" (Galatians 5:5).* Thus, how we live matters. In fact, according to Paul, how we live is the key to how we are judged. Many Evangelicals will claim that it is the Spirit who aids us to live a life fleeing sin. This is accurate, but the Spirit does not override our consciousness and make us automatons. God works within us, and we make the conscious decision to get rid of sin with His aid. We know this is the case because Paul himself constantly warns Christians to flee from sin! Does this duality to our walk in Christ indicate we have *earned* our salvation? Absolutely not, God accepts us how we are, and we are saved by grace; He then aids us in escaping a life enslaved by darkness.

The best way for to summarize Paul's usage of faith and works is this: we are justified by our faith. Faith is an umbrella term for all that constitutes the first steps of becoming a Christian, including *faith, repentance, confession, and baptism.* All of this is done without earning anything; we are saved by grace alone and made a New Creation. God takes us as we are, broken creatures, and calls us into His Kingdom as a New Creation. Our sins are washed away, and we receive the gift of the Holy Spirit.

The next step, however, does include works and is linked to our salvation. For the New Testament salvation is a "already but not yet" event. We are already saved, yet we are still being saved. This process of "being saved" is called sanctification. Many would like to claim sanctification is separate from salvation, but that's not what the Scriptures teach. Sanctification is the process of ridding your life of sin and walking in Christ. This is the process by which God refines us through the power of the Holy Spirit. This process takes an entire lifetime. Sanctification is not only part of the salvation process (though different from justification), but it is also a process which one must *work toward* with God's aid.

Here are some passages which support this view of sanctification being a part of salvation, and works being essential to that process:

> *Therefore be imitators of God as beloved children. And walk in love, as Christ loved us and gave himself for us, a fragrant offering and sacrifice to God. But sexual immorality and*

all impurity or covetousness must not even be named among you, as is proper among saints. Let there be no filthiness nor foolish talk nor crude joking, which are out of place but instead let there be thanksgiving. For you may be sure of this, that everyone who is sexually immoral or impure, or who is covetous (that is an idolater), has no inheritance in the kingdom of Christ and God (Ephesians 5:1-5).

Paul is speaking to Christians here and warning them to flee from such things as crude jokes and sexual immorality. He is warning them for a reason. That reason is because they can lose their salvation. In order for them to flee such sins they must make a conscious effort and seek aid through the Holy Spirit. This is not a "one sin and you are done" theology, but, rather, this verse stresses the importance that Christians must strive to live a life faithful to Christ.

Abide in me, and I in you. As the branch cannot bear fruit by itself, unless it abides in the vine, neither can you, unless you abide in me. I am the vine; you are the branches. Whoever abides in me and I in him, he it is that bears much fruit, for apart from me you can do nothing. If anyone does not abide in me he is thrown away like a branch and withers;

and the branches are gathered, thrown into the
fire, and burned (John 15:4-6).

Jesus here teaches us that in order for us to bear fruit (good works), we must abide in Him. This is equivalent to Paul's teachings in the aforementioned passages: we work out our own salvation (sanctification) and God aids us in this. Jesus also states that those who abide in Him but do not produce fruit are cut off from Him and burned. Do works matter? Yes, we must strive to follow Christ. Is it possible to be in Christ and refuse to grow/produce fruit? Yes, and there are dire consequences if we do so. We must make a conscious decision to live for Him each and every day.

FIVE

What Now?

For those who are still reading, and who have a conviction that they have been wrong about baptism in the past, there is still a difficult step ahead. What will you do now that you see the truth? In reference to our introductory example, the sky really is blue! Baptism really is for the forgiveness of sins, despite the possibility of you hearing differently for an entire lifetime. You have two routes to follow now. Firstly, you can deceive yourself and ignore the evidence as if it is not there. You can pretend as if all of this is simply too difficult for you to understand, hiding behind your own pronounced ignorance. That is a cowardly option. You have seen the evidence that baptism really is essential. The second, better route is for you to make a commitment to accept that the sky is blue (baptism is for the forgiveness of sins). Your shades have been removed; now, what follows is removing the shades from others. This could result in your very own family members spurning you. Many so-called preachers and teachers believe that anyone who calls baptism essential has "fallen from grace." This means that you could be seen as a heretic by many in your own religious circles. I would remind you that even Jesus was rejected, shamed, and nailed to a cross by the religious elite of His own culture. What should you do now? You should stand up for truth as Christ did and set the example. Make the decision now to follow this teaching no matter where it leads you.

Some of you are reading now and recognizing not only that baptism is essential, but also that you have yet to be baptized. To those at this point I will respond, "What are you waiting for?" as Paul was asked before his baptism (Acts 22:16). You have no excuse, get it done. Follow the example of the Ethiopian Eunuch in Acts 8:36 when he said, "See here is water. What prevents me from being baptized?" To the religious leaders and preachers, I remind you that it is your responsibility to practice baptism the right way. Many churches today wait weeks and months before ever baptizing a new believer. The baptisms are often performed all in one day with a multitude of people being immersed one after the other. This practice is not Biblical. There is not a single case of a person delaying their baptism in the New Testament. Baptism needs to be done as soon as possible for anyone who accepts Christ as Lord. Again, to the religious leaders, preachers, etc, it is your responsibility to make sure members understand the true purpose of baptism. It is for the forgiveness of sins. The doctrine of baptism needs to be practiced and taught the right way. There is no excuse for those who know the truth, but do not practice the truth. Fear of being fired or ridiculed is no excuse for salvific issues. Baptism is not a symbol of a salvation received once someone believes. Baptism is the moment a believer is saved and puts on Christ, receiving the indwelling presence of the Spirit.

What if a person is baptized but does not affirm that baptism is for the forgiveness of sins? Does this baptism still save? This question is of great importance. It saddens me to state that the tradition of with which I am familiar often falters when it comes to this question. It is claimed by many in this tradition that a person MUST understand what their baptism is for or it doesn't count. This excludes all who confess Jesus' name but are in error when it comes to the exact meaning of baptism. This thinking condemns most, if not all, Christians from the period of about the 6th century to the 19th century when the restoration movement began. This should be intolerable to even consider, but in many circles, it is the predominant thought. How can some claim that the church vanished in this way?

In Matthew 16:18 Jesus said: *"And I tell you, you are Peter, and on this rock I will build my church, and the gates of hell shall not prevail against it"*. Did Jesus say that His church would disappear for nearly a thousand years and then reappear with Alexander Campbell leading the charge in America? No, he stated that the gates of hell would not prevail against it. What Jesus started did not simply vanish. It is not only many restorers who make such condemning claims like this, but also many evangelicals who claim that accepting baptism as vital for forgiveness causes one to lose grace.

A person is saved at baptism based on faith in Christ, rather than perfect Bible knowledge. If a person is baptized for a Biblical reason in obedience to God, then I affirm that they are saved. The emphasis lies in believing that Christ is the Son of God rather than understanding baptism perfectly. Is understanding what baptism is for important? Absolutely. Why else would so many Scriptures affirm its importance? Baptism encompasses God's plan to save and there is beauty in His plan. It is important because many believers have died having never been baptized because no one ever told them it was essential.

We will now take a look at why some restorers claim that a person must be baptized knowing that their baptism is "for the forgiveness of sins." This idea comes from Acts 2:38 where Peter says, *"Repent and be baptized every one of you in the name of Jesus Christ for the forgiveness of your sins, and you will receive the gift of the Holy Spirit."* This passage is interpreted in two different ways. Firstly, it is interpreted that we should be baptized so that we receive the forgiveness of sins. This was my natural interpretation of the text for many years before realizing people were interpreting this a different way. This interpretation is what we will call the "blessing" interpretation. The second interpretation is what I am calling the "command" interpretation. This interpretation states that Peter was commanding them to be baptized a specific way. This means they are to be baptized with knowledge of what baptism is for and that all should be under the impression that this baptism is for the forgiveness of sins. This could also be seen when a person utters, "I baptize you for the forgiveness of sins" during the process. This entire debate is about what exactly Peter meant when he said, "for the forgiveness of sins." Is Peter's usage of the word "for" a command or blessing? I am not arguing about baptism here. Baptism is clearly both a command and a blessing, this debate centers completely around the word "for" here in Acts 2:38. Is the word "for" a *command* or the *explanation of a blessing* received when one is baptized. Meaning is Peter telling us how to be baptized, or what happens when we are baptized. Must we be baptized knowing it is "for" the forgiveness of sins or it does not count? Or was Peter here stating that we should be baptized "for" in that moment we will receive the forgiveness of sins?

The word "for" can be used in two different scenarios and mean two different things. If I said, "Go to the grocery store *for* a gallon of milk, and I'll give you ten bucks," then the usage of the word "for" here would be a command. The person is to go the grocery store to get milk. If, however, I said, "Eat protein *for* better nutrition, and you will live longer", then the word "for" here is simply stating what will happen if you eat protein. You will receive a blessing in that you will receive better nutrition. The better choice for these two interpretations is that Peter was explaining that baptism would result in the forgiveness of sins rather than trying to somehow command us to include the "forgiveness of sins" in the baptism ceremony. What would the command interpretation even look like in practice? Intellectual assent at the time of immersion? The words, "I baptize you for the forgiveness of sins" being uttered? The Scriptures reveal that baptism is when our sins are washed away, but no such formula exists in the New Testament as to what words ought to be uttered. For God to hold us to this standard we would need more instructions.

When it comes to the word "for," there is no way to tell exactly what Peter meant in Acts 2:38. It could be interpreted as either a command or blessing, although the blessing interpretation seems more obvious in the context. If the interpretation of command is true, then that means all who have been baptized without knowing what it was "for" are condemned to hell. This exclusion results in many Christians trying to convert the Baptists (or any other denominational persons) rather than reaching unbelievers. If the interpretation of blessing is true, then those who receive baptism still receive the blessing whether they realize precisely what it is for or not (the forgiveness of sins). When we step away from the text and we think about this philosophically and theologically, it becomes much easier. Do we serve a God who condemns based off of a triviality such as this? Is God more concerned with our knowledge of the sacraments or with our obedience and knowledge of Him? That question is easy; *Hosea 6:6 says: "For I desire mercy, not sacrifice, and acknowledgment of God rather than burnt offerings".* God cares more about who we are on the inside, morally, than He does about our exact ceremonial procedures. Burnt offerings were still necessary in the Old Law, but God revealed that mercy and knowledge of God was more important. We do not serve a "tricked-ya" God. God is not a joker and He is not trying to trick us into going to hell. Truly, those who state a person must know exactly what their baptism is for are only leaning on one specific possible (yet unlikely) interpretation of Acts 2:38. The average believer is not a Biblical/Theological scholar. The average believer is convicted of his or her sin, and simply wants to obey God. He or she may not know what exactly the Lord's Supper is. He or she may not know if one should pray with his or her eyes open or closed. He or she also may not understand how exactly God saves through faith in Christ. All one often knows is that he or she believes in Him and wants to follow Him and is willing to do that in baptism as He has commanded. That is enough. Jesus does not require of us to be Bible scholars to obtain salvation. The emphasis is on Him, not in how much we know. This is a rebuke not only towards many restorers, but also many evangelicals who, on the other side, state that a person must believe their salvation is based on "belief alone" or they are lost. If salvation is based on one's personal doctrinal stances within Christianity, then all will be lost. I have studied Scripture long enough to realize that, in five years, I will look back at some of my beliefs now and they will simply be wrong. No one has perfect Bible knowledge, and no one will ever have perfect Bible knowledge. Luckily, we are saved by grace not by works so that no one may boast. We are saved by Jesus and the emphasis is on Him.

It is interesting that many followers of the Restoration movement resist this "blessing" interpretation of Acts 2:38. "A person must know what their baptism was for or it didn't count!" they claim, yet fail to realize that the leading member of the Restoration movement is lost according to this logic. Alexander Campbell was baptized in 1812 by a Baptist preacher named Matthias Luce.[36] This preacher did not believe baptism was for the remission of sins. Not only did the preacher not believe this was baptism's purpose, but neither did Alexander Campbell at the time. Campbell decided to be immersed after realizing that sprinkling was not the Biblical model for baptism. The Restoration movement did not begin until 1827 when the first "remission of sins" baptism was performed (outside of the first 4 centuries of the church).[37] Alexander Campbell was a part of this movement, but he was not baptized in such a way, and no record exists of him ever being rebaptized.

Another leading member of the Restoration movement was David Lipscomb. Lipscomb did not believe a person was lost if they did not understand precisely the purpose of baptism. In Lipscomb's book *Salvation from Sin,* he writes of a question he received regarding a woman who did not know precisely the reason behind her baptism. His answer to the

---

[36] Smith, C. A. and Tant, J. D., "Smith-Tant Debate on "Campbell's Baptism": Was Alexander Campbell Baptized In Order to Obtain Remission of Sins?" (1936). Stone-Campbell Books. 12.

[37] Smith, C. A. and Tant, J. D., "Smith-Tant Debate on "Campbell's Baptism": Was Alexander Campbell Baptized In Order to Obtain Remission of Sins?" (1936). Stone-Campbell Books. 12.

question of whether or not she was saved was this, "Who dare say that she was not pardoned because she did not see that her baptism was for the remission of sins?"[38] This is the correct response. The woman was baptized because God commanded it. That was the only knowledge she had, and the only knowledge she needed. When Christians try to make up rules and regulations for what makes a baptism acceptable, they sin. It causes God to appear differently than He is. It makes Him look to be the God of the technicality, or a God who cares about all trivial matters. Believers who hold to these technicalities create an atmosphere that leads to folks feeling like they are walking on eggshells any time they are near a church building. One wrong move and they are chastised, or worse, God will smite them down immediately. This is not an accurate picture of the loving and merciful Father we serve! The Pharisees approached God's Law in the same way. They tried to put a hedge around His law. They created their own laws in order to ensure the people would not accidentally break one of God's actual laws. The result was a sharp rebuke from Jesus *(Matthew 23:4): "They tie up heavy burdens, hard to bear, and lay them on people's shoulders, but they themselves are not willing to move them with their finger."*

---

[38] David Lipscomb, and J. W. Shepherd. *Salvation from Sin.* Indianapolis, IN: McQuiddy Publishing Company, 1913, 227.

WHAT ABOUT MY FAMILY MEMBER?

This question always arises when a person learns the truth of baptism, "What about my grandfather who believed in Jesus, but was never baptized. Is he lost?" This question stops many Christians from ever accepting that baptism is for the remission of sins. The question is important, however. How will God handle those who lovingly followed Him in life but, due to deception, were never baptized? Technically speaking, we could not call such a person a Christian. It is at baptism that a person receives the Holy Spirit, receives forgiveness, and puts on Christ. This is the Christian model for how God saves humans, but sometimes God's models are broken, and He makes exceptions.

One of the most common objections to baptism is, "Well what about the thief on the cross?" This objection is not without merit. Jesus told the thief *(Luke 23:43) "today you will be with me in paradise."* The thief had no opportunity to be baptized, yet still he was saved. Jesus has the right to forgive anyone's sins however He sees fit. Many Christians object to this argument by quoting Hebrews 9:16-17 which says: *"For where a will is involved, the death of the one who made it must be established. For a will takes effect only at death, since it is not in force as long as the one who made it is alive."* The point is that the New Covenant was not in place until the shedding of blood happened, which was after Christ's death. The passage points out that the New Covenant did not emerge until Christ shed His blood. While that is certainly accurate, Jesus still inaugurated His Kingdom as He walked the earth, beginning the process of forgiving sins and changing the Covenant between Himself and humanity. The Hebrew writer's point was not that people were under the Old Covenant up until the exact moment Christ stopped breathing. Christ started *His* work of establishing *His* covenant during *His* lifetime, and His work came unto completion at His death when He said, "it is finished." To those who want to be technical on this point concerning the New Covenant not starting until the exact moment Jesus died, then I ask this: Was John's baptism not essential too? Those who claim that baptism was not necessary until the New Covenant are also forgetting that John the Baptist came baptizing for the forgiveness of sins (though not in Jesus' name), and Jesus sent His disciples to baptize people. At best, what can be said is that during Jesus's ministry and life on the earth there was a limbo taking place over what is acceptable to God in terms of His New Covenant. The thief on the cross is an example of God being God. God can forgive sins and work outside of the technicality. The thief on the cross was God forgiving sins outside of the New Testament model which includes baptism.

Let's explain what exactly is meant by technicality

and its relation to law. If I am driving 56 miles per hour in a 55 mile per hour zone, then, technically speaking, I have broken the speed limit. There are absurd-yet-funny stories of folks getting pulled over in such scenarios, but surely a good officer would not give someone a ticket over such a technicality, right? The vast majority of the time, a person can drive 1 mile per hour over the speed limit and be fine. There is a general consensus that no one can follow the speed limit so perfectly. The spirit of the law is still there, however, in that we need to drive around 55 miles per hour in that zone. The letter of the law states that a person has broken the speed limit (though only by 1 mile per hour). The spirit of the law, however, states that while technically speaking the letter was broken, the actual spirit of the law was not broken, that being the reason the law was put in place.

We live in a flawed, but necessary, judicial society. We are innocent until proven guilty. Within in our law system those who are charged with a crime must be proven guilty through the court of the law. Sadly, some criminals fall through the cracks based off of a technicality, despite others knowing they are guilty. A murderer could be caught on camera and his fingerprints could be recovered from the murder weapon, but if a detective makes a mistake at the crime scene, the whole case could be nullified, all due to a technicality. If a detective searches a criminal's car without permission or a search warrant, then the evidence he finds cannot be used in the court of law, no matter how incriminating. This is a technicality. These technicalities and rules must be set in a human judicial setting because without them judges and men in power could abuse their authority; the innocent could be wrongly convicted. Such technicalities in the law are not necessary, however, when we speak of a holy, good, and perfect Judge. When it comes to the technicality, we need to let God be God.

In Acts 10, we see another example of God working outside of His model and the technicality. Peter had just been sent to the house of Cornelius after God instructed him to preach the gospel even to the Gentiles. As Peter began preaching the gospel to these Gentiles, the Holy Spirit was poured out on all of them, and they spoke in tongues, extolling God. They had received the Holy Spirit and were speaking in tongues before baptism! Many read from this passage that baptism is not essential. This is error, as it is simply an example of God working outside of His model. Peter is even shocked that this happened and declares *(Acts 10:47): "Can anyone withhold water for baptizing these people, who have received the Holy Spirit just as we have?"* Peter's immediate response is to immerse these believers. Were these Gentile believers considered saved Christians before baptism? It most certainly seems to be that they were "saved" before baptism. The indwelling presence of the Spirit is the determining factor of a person's salvation, and they had received the Holy Spirit just as Peter had. Did Peter take from this example and then never baptize a Christian again? Of course not. Yet, many people read this passage and claim that baptism is not necessary.

The last example of God working outside of the technicality includes Jesus, God's own Son. Jesus knew the law better than any other man who walked the earth. After Jesus' baptism, He was tempted by Satan, and Satan quoted the Psalms out of context to deceive Jesus. Albeit, Satan failed every time. Jesus responded with Scripture of His own in each defense. Jesus understood the Scriptures perfectly, yet His understanding of them was much different than the understanding of the religious elite who studied them daily. The Pharisees and Scribes knew the letter of the law, but they failed to recognize the spirit of the Law. The religious elite could recite every rule and detail of the Scriptures. Their interpretations were so safe that they even built a law of their own on top of the original law.

The Scriptures revealed that work on the sabbath was forbidden. *Leviticus 23:3 reads: "Six days shall work be done, but on the seventh day is a Sabbath of solemn rest, a holy convocation. You shall do no work. It is a Sabbath to the LORD in all your dwelling places".* A person is not to work on the Sabbath. It is a simple command from God. What is interesting, however, is how Jesus approaches and understands the law. His understanding is radically different from the Pharisees and many Christians today.

> *One Sabbath he was going through the grainfields, and as they made their way, his disciples began to pluck heads of grain. And the Pharisees were saying to him, "Look, why are they doing what is not lawful on the Sabbath?" And he said to them, "Have you never read what David did, when he was in need and was hungry, he and those who were with him: how he entered the house of God, in the time of Abiathar the high priest, and ate the bread of the Presence, which it is not lawful for any but the priests to eat, and also gave it to those who were with him?" And he said to them, "The Sabbath was made for man, not man for the Sabbath. So the Son of Man is lord even of the Sabbath" (Mark 2:23-28).*

Many falter when interpreting this passage. They struggle, attempting to explain how Jesus did not break the law here. Technically speaking, Jesus did break the law. What I mean is that Jesus broke the *letter* of the law. Jesus broke the traditional, legalistic interpretations of the Pharisees, but He did not break the spirit of the Law. God did not create the Law of the Sabbath as a means of restricting people from doing necessary and good deeds in extreme cases. God surely is not angered if someone saves a person from a terrible injury on the Sabbath, or, as in Jesus' case, for a person to pluck corn from a field to feed himself when he is hungry. The problem is that such explanations of God fall on deaf ears to those who are slaves to the technicality. Jesus himself, in defense of His actions, mentions David and how David entered the house of God and ate the bread of the Presence. This was not a lawful act by David. David broke the letter of the Law here, but Jesus implies that David was not breaking the spirit of the Law.[39]

There is plenty of evidence in Scripture to suggest that we do not serve the God of the technicality. God has given us laws and guidance through the Scriptures. We need to follow them as precisely as we can, but we cannot allow ourselves to get lost in the minor details. Suppose a man experiences a plane crash in a desert. He is the lone survivor, and all he has available to him is a couple of water bottles and a Bible. In desperation, he reads the words of Jesus and the book of Acts. He knows he is going to die alone in the desert, but he has a Hope of salvation. He sees that he needs to be

---

[39] Shelly, Divorce and Remarriage: A Redemptive Theology, (Leafwood Publishing,:Abilene, TX, 2007) 38.

immersed for the forgiveness of sins, but no water is around except that of his last water bottle. He prays to God and asks for forgiveness. He declares belief in Jesus as the Son of God. He then pours the last bit of water on his head in hopes that it will be serviceable to God. Is such a man saved? Similar situations are often brought up in the discussion of the necessity of baptism. Unfortunately, I have witnessed this answered the wrong way too many times! We do not serve the God of the technicality. He can use that little bit of water to save this lonely desperate man in the desert. Even if the man didn't have any water, we serve the God who could still save Him just as Jesus saved the thief on the cross. We know who God is, and we know His character. I love the story of Samson. Samson was a man used by God, and his power came from God. God used Samson's hair, a physical element, to give Samson a spiritual blessing. It was through Samson's hair that he had incredible strength. Samson lost this strength, however, when Delilah cut off his hair. Was Samson's strength from His hair or from God? The only answer to such a question is: both! God worked through Samson's hair to give him strength. Why did God use hair? That can't be answered. Why does God use water today? That can't be answered. Samson's eyes were horrifically gouged out once his strength was gone, and he was made to work as a slave. As time passed, the text reveals that Samson's hair began to grow again. We do not know how much his hair had grown back, but the time that passed couldn't have been very long, for they brought Samson into their assembly to entertain them as they offered sacrifices to their god, thanking the idol for delivering Samson into their hand. It was in this assembly, as Samson was being mocked by thousands of Philistines (God's enemy), that he prayed and asked God *(Judges 16:28)*: *"O Lord God, please remember me and please strengthen me only this once, O God, that I may be avenged on the Philistines for my two eyes."* Samson, for the first time in Scripture's portrayal of his life, prayed to God for strength. His strength did not come naturally to him anymore from his long hair, but instead it came miraculously from God. Samson pushed the pillars down, killing himself and thousands of Philistines. God worked with what little bit of hair that Samson had on his head as he was imprisoned. Samson likely didn't even recognize that his hair had grown back. He simply pleaded to God for the strength and God provided. God could have acted the same way even if Samson's hair hadn't grown back at all.

As we close this discussion on technicalities let me be clear. I do not know if those believers who passed before me without baptism were saved. I believe that God has shown He is bigger than the technicality, and that He desires all to be saved. It is based on those two ideas that I believe some, at least, will still be saved.

I also understand this, however: God has made His model clear to us. Baptism is essential and examples/ definitions of the practice fill the New Testament. Just as there are times in the Scriptures where God looks past the technicality, there are also times when He does not. Touching the Ark of the Covenant for example, had deathly consequences (2 Samuel 6:1-7). The reader needs to understand that knowing God's Will and not following it is a serious mistake, and one that God will not take lightly. If you aren't baptized, then what are you waiting for? There may still be hope for your lost ancestor, friend, or acquaintance. *That does not mean you should ignore God's will.*

There are so many students of Scripture who completely ignore the doctrine of baptism for the remission of sins due to not being able to stomach the consequences of such a doctrine. They can't stand the thought that their father, mother, sister or brother is lost due to dying without baptism. I believe what I have stated previously will be of comfort, but also understand something else. What would this lost father want you to do? Would your lost father want you to hide in self-deception? Would he want you to teach your children wrongly? Those are his grandchildren, after all. Understand that you have more knowledge than your ancestor, it is your job to move forward in the future with the truth, rather than staying stuck in the past with deception.

I pray God will bless every reader who has dared to embark on this quest for Truth. The journey is over, and all that now awaits is a decision to be brave and confront the dragon. God promises to be with us. God is our Stronghold, and no matter what dangers await, we can always return to our loving Father for safety. Be bold with this newfound knowledge. Dare to think differently than the traditions of your heritage. Your shades are off, and now for the first time you see--with astonishment--that the sky is, actually, *blue*.

WORKS CITED

Balz, Horst, and Gerhard Schneider. Exegetical Dictionary of the New Testament, Vol 1, (Michigan: Eerdmans, 1978).

"Baptizo Meaning in Bible - New Testament Greek Lexicon - New American Standard." *Biblestudytools. com*,n.d.https://www.biblestudytools.com/lexicons/greek/nas/baptizo.html.

Cyprian of Carthage, *Dress of Virgins*. (As Cited by Ferguson, Eerdmans Publ.)

Cyprian of Carthage, Letters. (As Cited by Ferguson, Eerdmans Publ.)

Demonstration 3, translation by Joseph P. Smith, St. Irenaeus: Proof of the Apostolic Preaching, Ancient Christian Writers 16 (New York: Newman [Paulist],

1952, P.49. (As Cited by Ferguson, Eerdmans Publ.) (As cited by Ferguson, Eerdmans Publ.)

Exhortation 10.94.2., Clement of Alexandria. (As Cited by Ferguson, Eerdmans Publ.)

Ferguson, Everett. *Baptism in the Early Church: History, Theology, and Liturgy in the First Five Centuries.* Grand Rapids, Mich: W.B. Eerdmans Publ, 2009.

Instructor 1.6.50.4, Clement of Alexandria. (As Cited by Ferguson, Eerdmans Publ.)

Irenaeus, Fragment 34 (W. W. Harvey, Sancti Irenaei Libros quinque adversus haereses [Cambridge, 1857; repr. Ridgewood, NJ: Gregg, 1965], #33). (As cited by Ferguson, Eerdmans Publ.)

John H. Armstrong, *Understanding Four Views on Baptism,* (Michigan: Zondervan, 2007).

Lipscomb, David, and J. W. Shepherd. *Salvation from Sin.* Indianapolis, IN: McQuiddy Publishing Company, 1913.

Lienhard, Joseph T. *Origen: Homilies on Luke,* Fragments on Luke, Fathers of the Church 94 (Washington: Catholic University of America Press, 1996).

Origen: Homilies on Joshua, Fathers of the Church

105, Translation by Barbara J. Bruce, (Washington: Catholic University of America Press, 2002). (As cited by Ferguson, Eerdmans Publ.)

Origen: Homilies on Joshua, Fathers of the Church 105, Translation by Barbara J. Bruce, (Washington: Catholic University of America Press, 2002). (As cited by Ferguson, Eerdmans Publ.)

Shelly, Rubel, Divorce and Remarriage: A Redemptive Theology, (Leafwood Publishers: Abilene, Texas, 2007).

Smith, C. A. and Tant, J. D., "Smith-Tant Debate on "Campbell's Baptism": Was Alexander Campbell Baptized In Order to Obtain Remission of Sins?" (1936). Stone-Campbell Books.

Tertullian, Baptism. (As Cited by Ferguson, Eerdmans Publ.)

The Epistle of Barnabas, Translated by J.B. Lightfoot. (As cited by Ferguson, Eerdmans Publ.) **http://www. earlychristianwritings.com/text/barnabas-lightfoot.html**.

The Shepherd of Hermas, Mandates 4.3.31.1-2, Translated by J.B. Lightfoot. (As cited by Ferguson,

Eerdmans Publ.) **http://www.earlychristian writings.com/text/shepherd-lightfoot.html**.

Theophilus, To Autolycus, translation by Marcus Dods. (As cited by Ferguson, Eerdmans Publ.) **https:// www.newadvent.org/fathers/02041.htm**.

Yevamot 47b, The William Davidson Translation. (As cited by Ferguson, Eerdmans Publ.) **https:// www.sefaria.org/Yevamot**.

https://www.desiringgod.org/interviews/is-baptism-necessary-for-salvation?fbclid=IwAR 2GpP522pKhFYZbZm13bZWZN3kMm71Qus vbSCyzgyzBeZZuq9jcttKLUeI

ACKNOWLEDGMENTS

I would like to acknowledge a dear friend of mine since the Middle School days. We have discussed the meaning of baptism numerous times over the years. He arose in me a desire to put all of my ideas on paper. This book was, in part, for him.

Thanks for reading!
Please add a short review on
Amazon and let me know
what you thought!

Printed in the United States
by Baker & Taylor Publisher Services